OFFICIAL VERSIONS

For Bill Austin

Best with

M

OTHER BOOKS BY MARK PAWLAK

Poems:

Richard Edelman & Mark Pawlak (West End Chapbook)
The Buffalo Sequence (Copper Canyon)
All the News (Hanging Loose)
Special Handling: Newspaper Poems New and Selected (Hanging Loose)

Anthologies Edited:

Present/Tense: Poets in the World (Hanging Loose)
Shooting the Rat: Outstanding Poems and Stories by High School Writers, Co-editor (Hanging Loose)
Bullseye: Stories and Poems by Outstanding High School Writers, Co-editor (Hanging Loose)
Smart Like Me: High School-Age Writing from the Sixties to Now, Co-editor (Hanging Loose)

OFFICIAL VERSIONS

Mark Pawlak

Hanging Loose Press
Brooklyn, NY

Published by Hanging Loose Press, 231 Wyckoff Street, Brooklyn, NY 11217-2208. All rights reserved. No part of this book may be reproduced without the publisher's written permission, except for brief quotations in reviews.

www.hangingloosepress.com

Printed in the United States of America
10 9 8 7 6 5 4 3 2 1

Hanging Loose Press thanks the Literature Program of New York State Council on the Arts for a grant in support of the publication of this book.

Cover art: "Read for Knowledge," 1996, by Arnold Mesches, acrylic on canvas, 66" x 76"
Cover design by Marie Carter

The author is grateful to the following publications, where versions of some of these poems first appeared: *Bogg, Curious Rooms, Exquisite Corpse, Fresh Ground, Global City Review, Hanging Loose, Lungfull!, Off The Coast, New American Writing, Skanky Possum, The Saint Anne's Review, Shampoo, Slipstream, The Village Rambler,* and *The World.* Several poems also appeared in the anthologies *The Best American Poetry 2006,* Billy Collins, Ed. (Scribner), and in *Present/Tense: Poets in the World* and *Voices of the City,* both from Hanging Loose Press.

Library of Congress Cataloguing-in-Publication Data available on request.

ISBN: 1-931236-59-3 (paperback)
ISBN: 1-931236-60-7 (cloth)

Produced at The Print Center, Inc. 225 Varick St., New York, NY 10014, a non-profit facility for literary and arts-related publications. (212) 206-8465

Contents

For Mary and Gianni

"The truth is rarely pure and never simple."

—Oscar Wilde

"Pessimism of the spirit; optimism of the will."

—Antonio Gramsci

"Take things as they are. Punch when you have to punch. Kick when you have to kick."

—Bruce Lee

Three Official Versions

CREDIBLE INFORMATION, 1999–2003

For Gary Trudeau

June 19, 1999

At the wedding of Prince Edward and Sophie Rhys-Jones
Sir Geoffrey Shakerley, official photographer,
observed a "feeling of euphoria"
as he snapped pictures in Windsor Castle
after the ceremony at St. George's Chapel.

He did allow that one official photograph
of the bride and groom, the assembled
members of their families, and foreign royals,
had to be doctored, because Prince William,
son of Prince Charles and the late Diana, Princess of Wales,
and second in line to the throne,
did not look happy enough.

January 1, 2000

The controversy over when the 20th century
ends and the 21st century actually begins
was stirred up when Arthur C. Clarke,
author of *2001: A Space Odyssey*, took issue
last year with people who called the year 2000
the start of the 3rd millennium. "Though some people
have difficulty grasping this," he'd noted,
"we'll have had only 99 years of this century
by January 1, 2000."

A sixth-century Roman monk
is responsible for the confusion.
Dionysius Exiguus, also known as Dennis the Short,
created the calendar still in use in most of the Western world.

But because Romans did not have the concept of zero,
his calendar started with the year "One."

September 13, 2001

Stung by suggestions that in delaying his return
to Washington on September 11th,
President Bush had hurt himself politically
White House press secretary Ari Fleischer
disclosed that Mr. Bush had argued
strenuously for his immediate return to the capital—
not once but twice: on the morning of the attacks
and again that afternoon—but, Mr. Fleischer said,
the Secret Service had vetoed the president's plan
as too dangerous.

February 26, 2002

The Office of Strategic Influence was established after September 11th
to counter fears that the United States was losing public support
overseas for its war on terrorism, particularly in Islamic nations.
Its object was to use the foreign news media and the Internet
to tell the American side of the story. Plans for the office included
ways to "coerce" foreign journalists and opinion makers
and to "punish" those who convey the wrong message.
"A lot of the world does not like America,"
one senior official had said, "and it's going to take
years to change their hearts and minds."

June 19, 1999

It was Prince Edward who thought
the image of his teenage nephew
needed alteration. "Prince Edward said
he didn't think Prince William looked
absolutely his best," the photographer explained,
"so we were able to digitally
put in another image of Prince William

from one of the other shots where he is
smiling and laughing."

January 1, 2000

The millennium mistake is a symptom
of the "dumbing down" of society,
according to *Science* writer Jeff DeTray.
"Too many people have come to believe
that *everything*—even a historical fact—
is a matter of opinion," he wrote.
"When children embrace the idea
that something is true if enough people believe it,
the incentive to pursue critical thinking,
education, and hard work begins to disappear."

But at the Center for Millennial Studies,
Stephen O'Leary disagreed: "I frankly think
that people who are self-appointed experts
in timekeeping and chronology and calendars," he said,
"should shut the hell up
and let people have their party."

September 13, 2001

President Bush spent the day of September 11th
traveling a zigzag route:
first from Sarasota, Florida
to Barksdale Air Force Base near Shreveport, Louisiana;
then from Shreveport
to Offutt Air Force Base in Omaha, Nebraska;
finally, from Omaha to Washington, D.C.,
arriving back in the capital at seven p.m., almost ten hours
after he had learned of the first attack.

February 26, 2002

The Office of Strategic Influence has now been ordered
to cease operations. Defense Secretary Donald H. Rumsfeld
made the announcement one day after President Bush
expressed amazement "about reading
some allegation that somehow our government
would never tell the American people the truth."
The president told Mr. Rumsfeld he was concerned
that irreparable harm would be done
if our military was suspected of spreading
false information with journalists abroad.

June 19, 1999

Sir Geoffrey's assistant, Robert Simpson,
corroborated that Prince William was in a
"jubilant mood" during the photo shoot,
but that just at the moment that particular picture was snapped,
he had looked away from the camera.

January 1, 2000

The 24-hour Y2K festivities were barely over
when the countdown clock outside Philadelphia's City Hall
was restarted. In Chicago, the Millennium Celebration
begun in January 1999, runs through December 2001.
The city's events coordinator, Jamey Lundblad, said that
        Chicagoans
celebrated "in a huge way this New Year's Eve,
and we're going to be celebrating next New Year's Eve as well,
and all the way through the year 2001."

September 13, 2001

President Bush was never "in hiding,"
asserted senior presidential advisor Karl Rove;
rather, he had delayed his return because of

"real and credible information"
that he was a target of the terrorists.
"We're talking about specific and chilling evidence,"
Mr. Rove said, "not vague suspicions."
Neither he nor press secretary Fleischer
offered reporters an explanation
why this was not made public earlier.

February 26, 2002

Asked whether he thought the controversy
surrounding the Office of Strategic Influence
has harmed the military's credibility,
Defense Secretary Rumsfeld replied, "I doubt it.
I hope not. If it has, we'll rebuild it."
Rumsfeld added that the military will in the future
continue to use information to its advantage
but will stick with deceiving only its enemies on the battlefield,
not the international media.
"There's a lot of things that we have to do,
and we will do those things," he said.
"We'll just do them in a different office."

Coda, May 6, 2003

White House spokesman Ari Fleischer today acknowledged
that President Bush had traveled to the carrier *Abraham Lincoln*
in the Pacific Ocean last week
via a small Navy plane
because he wanted to experience a landing
the way carrier pilots do,
and not because the ship—
as had at first been maintained—
was too far out at sea
for him to arrive by helicopter.

The president and his top aides had made
no secret of Mr. Bush's excitement
at landing on a carrier at sea
in a small plane traveling 150 miles per hour
and being brought to a halt by an arresting cable.
The decision to fly in the S3B Viking jet rather than a helicopter
was made by Mr. Bush himself. "The president wanted to land on it
in an aircraft that would allow him to see an aircraft landing
the same way that the pilots see an aircraft landing," Fleischer said.
"He wanted to see it as realistically as possible."

The White House spokesman denied
the accusations of Democratic opponents
that the President's decision to make a "Top Gun"-style entrance—
emerging from the four-seat jet, dubbed Navy One,
in a full flight suit with a helmet under his arm—
was in any way intended to turn the *Abraham Lincoln*, its crew
and fighter pilots returning home victorious from the Iraq war
into a prop for the President's re-election campaign.

A Boy's Life, 1960

For Gianni

Winter

Snowing all day & night. 3 hours
to deliver Sunday papers pulling sledge.
Read *Treasure Island* again.
Stained microscope slides:
fly wing, onion skin, dandruff. . . .

Glued balsa landing struts on Sopwith Camel.
Read *The Monitor and The Merrimack*.
Kielbasa soup & kidney pie!
Caught a puck in my eye playing hockey.
Got a shiner.

Shoveled driveway and sidewalk twice.
Sent for Edmond Scientific's catalog.
Listened to radio with earplug under covers;
Canisius vs. St. Bonaventure:
Bonnies 72 (Yay!) ; Griffs 67.

Another blizzard. No school.
Tobogganing at Chestnut Ridge Park.
Traded *Green Lantern* comics for *Fantastic Four*.
Read *Mysterious Island*. Up late
watching *Attack of the Fifty-Foot Woman*.

Snagged five perch ice fishing. Clipped ad
for authentic Bowie knife in *Boys' Life*.
Saw meteor shower. Waited up for Dad.
We watched *Late Night With Johnny Carson*.
Midnight snack: roast beef on wick!

Teamed up with Cousin Louie in doubles ping-pong.
Played Stratego. Mounted stamps in album.
Tried out for part in school pageant.
Landed role as Frederick Barbarossa. My costume:
a Knights of Columbus jacket, sword & scabbard!

Skating at Roosevelt Park rink.
Dad showed us how to "crack the whip."
Tried out for Immaculate Heart basketball team.
Read *Life on the Mississippi*.
Female swordtail looks pregnant.

   Spring

Painted candy-red stripe
on model '56 Mustang; added decals.
Bowled three strings, made 5 strikes.
The Day the Earth Stood Still—scary!
Ice breaking up on Niagara River.

Easter: Bopschu's sauerkraut pierogies
and duck's blood soup!
Played charades with cousins.
Learning Latin to be an altar boy (ugh).
30 situps, 16 pushups.

Baseball practice started. Threw out Mike C.
trying to steal second. Paper drive
to raise money for team uniforms.
Counted 19 baby guppies.
Chameleons & iguanas on sale in pet shop!

Biked to the abandoned quarry.
Caught a black water snake. Let it go.
Found fern fossils, but no *trilobites*.
Target practice with bb gun.
Shagged fly balls.

Summer

Hitachi transistor radio for my birthday, plus
Stan "The Man" Musial autographed baseball.
Read *Hound of the Baskervilles.*
Swimming at Schiller Park. Split my gut
watching the *Red Skelton Show.*

Rode shotgun with Dad to Canada
over the Peace Bridge to buy fireworks.
Lit Roman candles & sparklers after dark
at Fourth of July cookout. The uncles
played poker wearing silly hats.

Mowed lawns, earned 2 bucks.
Later, ate "mistakes" at Uncle Fred's Dairy Queen.
Dove from the high board at Schiller Park pool
and didn't belly flop once. Shagged fly balls.
Demolition Derby at War Memorial Stadium.

Biked to fishing hole; jigged for "bullheads."
Sat in the bleachers at Offerman Stadium. Saw
Luke Easter hit two balls over the left field fence.
People watching the game from their rooftops.
Journey to the Center of the Earth at Airport Drive-in.

Hooray for *Wildroot Charlie!*, first across the finish line
at hydroplane races on the Niagara.
Traded baseball cards: got Whitey Ford, Tony Kubek.
Played Wiffle Ball "Strike Out" until dark. Len L.
caught a 30 lb. muskie beyond the harbor breakwall!

Prorok family picnic at Schlegel's farm:
picked corn, trapped salamanders,
played softball & Capture the Flag.
Twisted my ankle climbing Akron Falls,.
Invasion of the Body Snatchers on *Late Night Movie.*

Sunday drive to Niagara Gorge.
Saw the whirlpool. Saw the barrels.
Played "French and Indian War" at Fort George.
Rode the Crystal Beach roller coaster
three times and never got sick!

Labor Day to Mel & Rene's cottage on the lake.
Trolled from outboard, hooked a pike.
Played miniature golf at Sunset Beach Amusement Park.
Tossed horseshoes. Roasted corn in a barrel.
Uncle Ed taught me Marine holds.

Autumn

Raked & bagged leaves, earned 2 bucks.
Took bow & arrow target practice.
67 daily papers, 156 Sunday.
Bought new tires and headlight for my bike.
Venison is tough to chew and tastes gamy.

Gathered horse chestnuts. Played "Kingers."
Read *Microbe Hunters* again.
Ate roast pheasant that Uncle Joe bagged.
Mom teaching me to fox trot & polka.
She says I have "two left feet."

Home sick from school four days.
Read *The Lewis and Clark Expedition.*
Read *Trappers and Traders of the Far West.*
Read *Kit Carson and the Wild Frontier.*
Read *Teddy Roosevelt and the Rough Riders.*

Counted Christmas tips. Rolled pennies from jar.
Waited up for Dad on New Year's Eve.
We ate pickled herring and pig's knuckles together.
Heard Guy Lombardo and his Royal Canadians
on the TV play "Auld Lang Syne."

HART'S NECK HAIBUN: TENANTS' HARBOR, MAINE

Book I: 2000

July 24

. . . three horses, two dogs (Muggins and Sport), one carriage, three cases of wine, two packages of stovepipe, two stoves, one iron pot, four washstands, one barrel of hardwood, seventeen cots, seventeen mattresses, four canvas packages, one buckboard, five large barrel and one half-barrel. Two tubs of butter, one bag of coffee, one chest of tea, a crate of china, a dozen rugs, four milk cans, two drawing boards, twenty-five trunks, thirteen small boxes, a boat, and a hamper. . . .

Each summer we promise ourselves we'll pack less!

July 25

We arrive at Hart's Neck in hard, driving rain. There are three parked cars blocking the path to Maplewood Cottage. Numerous corpulent adults and a six-month-old baby are inside tiny, two-room Birch next door. How do they all fit?

The "man of the house" arrives later—the others, now gone, were relatives down for the weekend. In contrast to his wife's girth, he is skinny as a rail, has a nervous tick, and is weighted down by an enormous ring of keys, dangling on a chain from his belt. (Mary: "Are you sure he's not a speed freak?").

July 26

Parked in a field
off the road to Owl's Head,
the same, weathered
late model sedan
· as last summer—no,
since the summer before that!

Grown up around it, hood-height,
now as before: goldenrod,
purple loosestrife,
black-eyed Susans,
Queen Anne's lace.

July 27

The neighbors in Birch are down from Vermont: the husband, C.,
is a carpenter/handyman, here on a working vacation, building
a studio for Ken Noland, a famous artist who is relocating from
north woods to coast. The wife, A., stays at the cottage all day
with baby, or strolls the rocky shell-strewn beach below our porch
when the tide is out. She invites Gianni to join her, introduces
him to taunting crabs: crack open a mussel, drop the meat into
the water between the seaweed-enwigged rocks, then wait. Soon
rock crabs emerge to fight over the scraps. Woman and boy are
endlessly entertained!

July 28

Deep rumble and thrum
of a lobster boat motor
rattles my sleep at 4 a.m.
Dream falls to the plank floor,
shatters.

July 29

A. tells Mary that the third cottage, now vacant, had been occupied by unfriendly folks who made a loud show of slamming doors and shutting windows, locking the cabin up tight each time they left for an excursion to beach or town. They packed up and departed abruptly the day before we arrived.

July 30

> Buzzing mosquito
> that worried my sleep
> turned out to be a
> distant outboard motor—
> and now it is dawn.

July 31

C., the carpenter, returns at dinnertime just as the fog rolls in, pops open a beer can, lifts the baby to the sky, plops himself down in a rocking chair on his porch overlooking the harbor. Quiet, then suddenly, there is a loud whistle and whoosh followed by a bang. Bottle rockets! He's setting off bottle rockets from the porch!

Gianni: "What do bottle rockets look like, Dad?"
Mary: "Gianni, you stay indoors."
Me: "The guy's just letting off steam."
Mary: "Now we know why their neighbors locked all the doors and windows."

August 1

Under cover of fog, someone has ironed smooth the wind-wrinkled waves. The harbor now flat as the plate glass atop my boyhood bureau. Resting on it: toy boats of varied colors, shapes, sizes, their hulls and masts mirrored below:

Alpha Wolf

Arcturus

Amoret

Blue Moon

Easterly II

Equinox

Broken Leash

Diva

Green Arrow

Holy Mackerel!

Inspiration

Jade

Just Deserts

Katie

Lady Mary Day

Katrajena

Liberté

Kiva

Lively Mistress

Mea Sonho

Norah D

Northern Light

Sea Dancer

Sea Hawk

Sea Rose

Plain Jane

Sturdy Beggar

Sparkle Bright

Tequila Sunrise

Tipsea

Surprise

Tangent

Whistler

Viking

August 2

A down comforter
has descended
over harbor and shore

August 3

"Gray as the inside of a buckwheat pancake."

August 4

Fog Bank, Sand Bar, Fish School, Gull Stand, Clam Digs, Cloud
Laundromat, Tide Postmark . . .

August 5

White birches'
lichen-crusted trunks
climb out of sight;
their branches
tickle tears
from fog's hem.

August 6

"Glue-fingered dawn"

August 7

Milky, watery light.
Birches are the
photo negative of themselves,
their trunks as if
drawn in charcoal
and daubed with real snow,
their branches hung
with pale green ornaments.

August 8

"Beaten-metal bay." "Lit pewter lagoon."

August 9

Droplets—
a string of them—
hang the length of
the windowframe,
refract
what light there is

August 10

Fog has lifted,
so too our mood

August 11

Spiders throw nightly lawn parties. Mornings, I find their tent canopies still pitched in the mown grass of the side yard. Tiny lanterns strung along the fringes shimmer in dawnlight.

> *Gonna pitch a*
> *Wang dang doodle*
> *All night long*
> *All night long*

Grasshoppper days, cricket nights, spider web mornings....

Notes:
" . . . three horses, two dogs . . . " —from a family diary found at one of the Adirondack "Great Camps," circa 1900; quoted in Paul Schneider, *The Adirondacks*

"Gray as the inside of a buckwheat pancake." — from *The Diary of James Schuyler*, Nathan Kernan, editor.

"Glue-fingered dawn" —Charles North, "The Brooklynese Capital"

"Beaten-metal bay." "Lit pewter lagoon."—from *The Diary of James Schuyler*, Nathan Kernan, editor.

"Gonna pitch a . . . " —"Wang Dang Doodle," written by Willie Dixon, as sung by Koko Taylor.

All Shook Up

Do's and Don'ts

*Tony Bennett said it was Frank Sinatra who told him, "Steal
from one person and it's plagiarism. Steal from everybody and
it's research."*

"Keep a strict eye
on eulogistic &
dyslogistic adjectives,"
Lewis (C.S.) advised
Tynan (Kenneth).
"They shd *diagnose*
(not merely blame)
& *distinguish*
(not merely praise)."

"Almost any noun is better
alone than chaperoned
if it is the right noun,
and very few can stand
two adjectives"—Pound
to Parker Tyler, '35—
"'Unsettled dream'
is stronger than
'unsettled white dream'."

Precision and economy of language
are virtues this author (me) recommends
when writing poems,
but finds difficult
to put into practice.

"It's more important,"
Ornette Coleman once said,
"to play the correct
feeling
than the correct note."

"Some of the time,"
to quote Chuck Close,
"you know you're cooking;
the rest of the time,
you just do it."

Or as the handbook
on improvisation
for church organ advises:
"Do not be afraid
of being wrong;
just be afraid of being
uninteresting."

DOUBLE FEATURES

The Deer Hunter
Dances With Wolves

*

Bonnie and Clyde
The Best Years of Our Lives

*

Snow White and the Seven Dwarfs
Birth of A Nation

*

The Sound of Music
All Quiet on the Western Front

*

Double Indemnity
Butch Cassidy and the Sundance Kid

*

Guess Who's Coming to Dinner
Frankenstein

From "The 100 Best American Movies"

MATCHINGS: BRITISH AUTHORS, 1343-1928

"We have really everything in common with America nowadays except, of course, language."

—Oscar Wilde

A	B
Austen	Academy
Blake	Auctioneers
Byron	Auto Country
Browning	Bargain Center
Chaucer	Boutiques
Clare	Bow Hut
Coleridge	Cooks for You
DeQuincy	Corner Ice Cream Parlor
Dickens	Corporate Conditioning Body-Building Gyms
Dryden	Dairy Queen
Goldsmith	Drapery Service
Hardy	Drive Thru Express
Hobbes	Elevator
Hopkins	Estates
Johnson	Fas Chek
Keats	Hitching Post
Marlowe	House of Pizza
Marvell	Leather Corp.
Milton	Lock & Key
Pope	Mel-o-Cream Donuts
Rossetti	Mystery Bookstore
Shelley	Pastime Recreation
Spenser	Playcare
Southey	Quick Serv Market
Stevenson	Readability Lab
Swinburne	Rigging Loft
Thackeray	Table & Tap
Tennyson	Three Hair Studio
Wordsworth	Vision Clinic

SOLUTIONS: BRITISH AUTHORS, 1343-1928

Austen Lock & Key: 206 535-9791
Blake Estates: 617 364-5277
Browning's Bow Hut: 423 369-2521
Byron Cooks for You: 913 232-6535
Chaucer Leather Corp: 508 373-1566
Clare's Boutiques: 617 423-3880
Coleridge Elevator: 402 283-4247
DeQuincy Dairy Queen: 318 786-7972
Dickens' Corner Ice Cream Parlor: 810 437-9763
Dryden's Quick Serv Market: 513 544-3977
Goldsmith Auctioneers: 617 787-4433
Hardy'sAuto Country: 315 675-3006
Hobbes Corporate Conditioning Body-Building Gyms: 617 890-6667
Hopkins Hitching Post: 612 933-9649
Johnson's Three Hair Studio: 617 427-5911
Keats Bargain Center: 901 852-2117
Marlowe's Pastime Recreation: 919 478-3326
Marvell Vision Clinic: 501 829-3402
Milton Fas Chek: 304 743-3991
Pope Rigging Loft: 503 228-1426
Rossetti's Drive Thru Express: 614 471-8066
Shelley Drapery Service: 617 723-6150
Spenser's Mystery Bookstore: 617 262-0880
Southey House of Pizza: 617 268-8939
Stevenson's Mel-o-Cream Donuts: 217 528-2303
Swinburne Readability Lab: 804 296-1713
Tennyson Playcare: 817 776-0280
Thackeray's Table & Tap: 617 890-6656
Wordsworth Academy: 215 348-7625

TIPS

Do your candles get stuck
in the candle holders?
Use a cotton swab
and dab some petroleum jelly inside
before you put the candle in it.

A bit of petroleum jelly
rubbed gently into your cuticles
will soften them
and will help
your nails grow.

Rub your hands lightly with petroleum jelly
before you tackle a painting project.
When it is time to clean up,
the paint will come right off.

A dab of petroleum jelly
on a door hinge
will keep it
from squeaking.

A cotton ball
soaked in petroleum jelly
makes a great fire starter
when you are
out camping.

—Found: *Worcester Telegram & Gazette*

BABY

For Mary, "My Babe"

Baby Baby Don't Cry
Baby Blue
Baby Come Back
Baby Don't Go
Baby Hold On
Baby I Need Your Loving
Baby That's It
Baby Won't You Please

Baby
Baby

Baby Get it On
Baby I Love You
Baby It's You
Baby Let's Play House
Baby Love
Baby Talk
Baby Workout
Baby You're Right

Baby
Baby Baby

Boogie Woogie Baby
Come On Baby
Don't Cry Baby
Kissa Me Baby
Love My Baby
Stick With Me Baby
Weep No More My Baby
You're My Baby

Baby Baby
Baby Baby

Be-Bop Baby
Goodtime Baby
Hully Gully Baby
Million Dollar Baby
Oh Baby
Tell Me Pretty Baby
Yes Baby
You Baby

Baby
Baby Baby
Baby Baby Baby

From: *Billboard's American Rock 'n' Roll in Review*

ALL SHOOK UP

For Dick Lourie

Baby Don't Do It
Cross Over the Bridge
Dance With Me
Earth Angel
For What It's Worth
Gangster of Love
Hard Headed Woman
I Almost Lost My Mind
Just Walkin' in the Rain
Last Night
My Heart Has a Mind of Its Own
Needles and Pins
Over, Under, Sideways, Down
Pain in My Heart
Quarter to Three
Reconsider Baby
Shakin' All Over
Talk Talk Talk
Um, Um, Um, Um, Um, Um
Voo-It Voo-It
What Kind of Fool
You're A Heart Breaker

*

You're a Heart Breaker
What Does It Take
Untie Me
Tired of Waiting for You
Saturday Night
Ride Your Pony
Party Doll

Over And Over
Next Time You See Me
Mustang Sally
Laugh Laugh
Keep Walking On
Juke
I've Been Lovin' You Too Long
Honky Tonk Women
Greenback Dollar
Fun Fun Fun
Everything's All Right
Down on the Corner
Choo Choo Ch'Boogie
Blue Suede Shoes
Ain't Doin' Too Bad

ALLEY OOP

*"If anything can be said in prose, then poetry should be
saved for saying nothing"*

—Pierre Albert-Birot

Be-Bop-a-Lula
Bip Bam
Boogie Oogie Oogie
Bop Ting-a-Ling

> Sh'Boom
> Tick Tock
> Tutti Frutti
> Wah-Watusi

Bumpity Bump
Buzz-Buzz a-Diddle-It
Cha Cha Doo
Chica Boo

> Sh'Boom
> Tick Tock
> Tutti Frutti
> Wah-Watusi

Ching Chong
Choo Choo Ch'Boogie
Chug-a-Lug
Da Doo Ron Ron

> Sh'Boom
> Tick Tock
> Tutti Frutti
> Wah-Watusi

Diddle-Dee-Dum
Diddy Wah Diddy

Ding-a-Ling
Doo De Doo

    Sh'Boom
    Tick Tock
    Tutti Frutti
    Wah-Watusi

Doo Wah Diddy Diddy
Dum Dum
Giddy Up a Ding Dong
Heeby-Jeebies

    Sh'Boom
    Tick Tock
    Tutti Frutti
    Wah-Watusi

Hey Hey Hey
Hey Bob-a-Re-Bop
Hot Ziggity
Hully Gully

    Sh'Boom
    Tick Tock
    Tutti Frutti
    Wah-Watusi

Ka-Ding-Dong
Ko Ko Mo
Ling Ting Tong
Loop De Loop

    Sh'Boom
    Tick Tock
    Tutti Frutti
    Wah-Watusi

Louie Louie
Mau Mau

My, My, My
No, No,No

    Sh'Boom
    Tick Tock
    Tutti Frutti
    Wah-Watusi

Ob-La-Di, Ob-La-Da
Oh, Boy!
Ooby Dooby
Ooh La La La

    Sh'Boom
    Tick Tock
    Tutti Frutti
    Wah-Watusi

Ooh Poo Pa Doo
Oooh-Oooh-Oooh
Pappa-Oom-Mow-Mow
Peek-a-Boo

    Sh'Boom
    Tick Tock
    Tutti Frutti
    Wah-Watusi

Q-Bob She-Bop
Rag Mama Rag
Rama Lama Ding Dong
Run Run Run

    Sh'Boom
    Tick Tock
    Tutti Frutti
    Wah-Watusi

Sha Boop Sha Boop
Shake Shake Shake

Shimmy Shimmy Ko Ko Bop
Shoo-Doop-Shoo-Be-Doo

    Sh'Boom
    Tick Tock
    Tutti Frutti
    Wah-Watusi

Switch-a-Roo
Ta Ta
Ting-a-Ling
Tweedlee Dee

    Sh'Boom
    Tick Tock
    Tutti Frutti
    Wah-Watusi

Wang Dang Doodle
Well-a, Well-a
Wing Ding
Wooly Bully

    Sh'Boom
    Tick Tock
    Tutti Frutti
    Wah-Watusi

Yakety Yak
Yummy Yummy Yummy
Zippity Zum
Zu Zu Man

    Sh'Boom
    Tick Tock
    Tutti Frutti
    Wah-Watusi

Sh'Boom
Tick Tock
Tutti Frutti
Wah-Watusi

Book II: 2001

July 25

Clank of rigging against masts announces a blow. Gulls perched in a line along the dock rail all face into it, as do the prows of the boats anchored, berthed, moored in harbor, hulls rocking . . .

Acanthus   *Honey Dew*
Black Seal   *Barnabas*
Dragon Lady   *Island Girl*   *Portunatus*
Holy Sheet Mon   *Avocet*   *Ever Green*
                                                                Susan Jane

            Xanadu
            After Hours   *Nootka*
                                                                    Kayla Marie

        Born Free   *School Teacher*
                                    Historian's Craft   *Keelian*
                                    Seventh Sojourn   *Rutabaga*
                Chance

        Freelance
        Glass Slipper

Indigo
        Jane
                Katie
                    Marbella
                        Nellie
                                Rachel
                                    Sasha

                                        Stormwatch
                                        Surprise

July 26

A variation on the stiff breeze:
starched breeze
of this dazzling bright day,
the brilliant blue sky
scrubbed clean of clouds.

July 27

Night so black it's blue. Every star of the New/Postmodern
American Poetry is on display: Here below Arcturus (the star not
the boat) are the Beats; there beside Vega are the Black Mountain
poets; the New York School is gathered around Daneb (I prefer
"constellation" to "school" of writers); and, faintly visible above
the horizon, the Objectivists.

July 28

Slate-gray, smooth-
polished to a sheen,
becoming wind-dimpled,
then coaxed into
washboard ripples.
Here, there,
teases of meringue.

July 29

Dockside: dories, skiffs, and one Boston Whaler—all turned turtle.

July 30

Harborside rocking chair aesthetics:
the lines of this white dory,
riding high at its mooring
strike me as sexy this brilliant a.m.
Its shapely stern
's a turn-on.

July 31

My Dear, shall we rusticate this summer at The Anchorage or at The Breakers, at Billowview or at Fantasea, at Fogcutter or at Spindrift, at Spurwinkle, at Itsuitsus, or at Pakh-ya-kahkus?

August 1

Offshore,
moiling gulls
pester
two lobster boats
hauling traps.

On shore,
swarming gnats,
encircle
one sun-bronzed head
(mine).

August 2

" . . . you can never be sufficiently alone when you write, there can never be sufficient silence when you are writing, night is even too little night."

August 3

Sky
the color of milk
that blueberries
have been in.

August 4

Additions to the catalog of breezes:
wrinkle-free breeze
relaxed fit breeze
permanent press breeze
wash-and-wear breeze
pressed & creased breeze.

August 5

"white flakes on a crawling sea. . . . "

August 6

"The thing that teases the mind over and over for years, and at
last gets itself put down rightly on paper. . . . "

August 7

"Chilly Saranwrap and aluminum foil days with beads of
moisture condensing on them."

August 8

"Part of my idea or my feeling about form that's interesting,"
says Fairfield Porter, "is that it is discovered—that it's the effect of
something unconscious like, you know, the dishes are in a certain
arrangement at the end of the meal because people without
thinking have moved things and then gone away. And I think it's
impossible not to get some sort of form if you don't think about it.
If you do think about it you can get chaos. But if you don't think
about it you get form."

"I want to write as well as I can, but I want to make some money at it. Thank God I'm not a poet."

*

"Dad, do you still work for Hanging Loose?"
> "Yes, I do. "
"You do your work at your office, right?"
> " No. Actually, I mostly do my Hanging Loose work at home."
"Oh?"
> "You see me stretched out on the couch reading fat
> envelopes full of poems. That's doing my Hanging
> Loose work."
"So you have two jobs?"
> "Yes, I guess you could say that, except that I don't get
> paid by Hanging Loose. I do it because I like to do it."
"Oh, OK."

*

"Be playful about work."

August 10

Mary: "Up since the crack of dawn! What have you been doing ?"
Me: "Stealing material from other people's notebooks."

" . . . anything that you can use, you should use it"

Notes:

My Dear, . . . : During the Gilded Age, wealthy visitors to
Mt. Desert from Boston, New York, Philadelphia were called
"Rusticators." They went to their "camps" and "cottages" to
commune with Nature, i.e. to "rusticate."

" . . . you can never be sufficiently alone when you write. . . . "
—Kafka, letter to Felice Bauer.

"the color of milk . . . "—Merrill Gilfillan, "Satin Street"

"white flakes on a crawling sea . . . "—Guy Davenport, *The Meadow Lark*

"The thing that teases the mind over and over . . . —Sarah Orne Jewett, letter

"Chilly Saranwrap. . . . "—from *The Diary of James Schuyler*, Nathan Kernan, editor

"I want to write as well as I can . . . "— Elmore Leonard

"Be playful about work."—Fairfield Porter

" . . . anything that you can use . . . "—Ted Berrigan, from a talk at Naropa, 1982

Wilson's Phalarope

Elephants Find Love

For Ron Schreiber, 1934–2004

The male and female Wilson's phalarope,
unlike other Alaskan shorebirds,
reverse typical parental roles.

Field ornithologists report
that it is the male phalarope
who shoulders the work
of incubating the eggs
and rearing the young.

As reported in the *Daily News* ,
normally monogamous
female penguins
at the New York Aquarium
are spending time
with males other than their mates.

The aquarium's ten
female black-footed penguins
are outnumbered by
twenty-two males,
and have been
taking advantage of it.

After depositing her eggs,
the female phalarope
leaves the nest
to court and mate
with other males;

but another
incubating male
will resist her advances
with head forward displays,
flying threats and pecks.

Aquarium spokeswoman Gina Fisher
said a penguin named Gomez
is the most sexually active female,
having up to four partners a day.

Gomez then returns
to the "home" she has shared
for three years
with her mate Giovanni.

2.

According to Darwin's theory
of sexual selection, male monkeys
should compete among themselves
for access to potential mates;

but in the mountains of Kyoto, Japan,
there lives a troupe
of one-hundred twenty macaques,
where the males do not
because the females are "lesbians."

Canadian primatologist Paul Vasey,
reports that these female macaques
reject male advances

in favor of a female partner
92.5 percent of the time.

3.

Asian elephant Kuhcharat
and his elephant bride Numvhan
(wearing bridal veil and ear-tassels
in the photograph above)
sit side by side during their
"wedding ceremony"
held yesterday in Thailand.

Breeders expect them to mate
and produce offspring.

THE SHARPER THE BERRY

Nose out of joint, City Slicker?
Blown a gasket, Hot Shot?
Fit to be tied, Arty Farty?
Going through the roof, Curtain Raiser?

Sometimes you get the bear, sometimes the bear gets you.

Can't put the toothpaste back in the tube, Clever Dick?
Chewing nails and spitting tacks, Front Runner?
Got your knickers in a knot, your panties in a wad, Sexy Thing?

Every rose has its thorn.

Popped a vein, Man-of-the-World?
Rubbed the wrong way, Lean-and-Mean?

Worse things happen at sea.

Worked into a lather, Bold-as-Brass?
Blood at a boil, Dressed-to-the-Nines?

It's not the end of the world.

Tomorrow is another day, All-Wind-and-Piss.
It's always darkest before the dawn, Bottom-of-the-Heap.
There is a light at the end of the tunnel, Thick-as-a-Brick.
Behind the clouds, the sun is shining, Back-to-the-Wall.
After the rain comes a rainbow, All-Work-and-No-Play.
Midnight is where the day begins, Beats-His-Meat.

Chin up! With visions of redemption,
walk against the crowd, Down-at-the-Heels.

If you can't enjoy your own company, how can anyone else, Drama Queen?

Everyone might hate you, but at least you're still alive, Button Pusher.

ACCORDING TO THE *TIMES*,

the bride wore layers
of used and hand-sewn clothing—
a salmon-colored underslip
with a ruffled hem,
a slinky flowery gown
she had made,
a pink sheer overslip,
a sheer bolero jacket
with a white fur collar,
and a rhinestone tiara.
"She looked," one guest said,
"like a princess
coming through the trees. . . . "

The bridegroom wore a lime-green suit
found at an apartment sale,
with two-toned loafers.
He could have been, said the article,
on a golf course in Las Vegas,
circa 1960.

"Never pay retail,"
the bride was overheard to say,
"that's one of the ten deadly sins."

AIMING HIGH

For Errol Morris

"I always thought that record would stand until it was broken."
—Yogi Berra

Sui Generis
Extreme sports enthusiast Wolfgang Kulov
has claimed a world record for cycling underwater
a distance of two and six-tenths miles
along the bottom of Germany's North Sea coastline.

Samir Tandon has his name featured
in the *Limca Book of Records*,
the Indian version of the *Guinness Book*
for his ability to recite songs
from Hindi language films backwards.

Paul Hunn is famous as the man who produced
the loudest burp ever measured,
a belch comparable in volume to a pneumatic drill
or to an aircraft taking off. And now,
he has set out to surpass his own record.

Bibhuti Bhushan Nayak , a martial arts expert
and man of numerous feats,
has made his latest mark in the groin smash,
in which three forty-one-pound blocks
were placed on his groin
then smashed with a sledgehammer.

Phenomenal
Wolfgang Kulov, who used a specially designed
lead bicycle for his underwater feat,
was followed by divers and by spectators
traveling on the surface in boats

from Scharbeutz, in Schleswig-Holstein,
to the Timmendorf beach,
in the neighboring German province of Ostseebad.

Besides film songs, Samir Tandon is also known to read out
entire passages from newspapers,
to recite verses from ancient Sanskrit texts,
and to repeat pieces of conversation he has just heard,
all in reverse.

Guinness World Records officials were on hand
with sound-level meters and recording equipment
to verify Paul Hunn's attempt to set a new burping mark.
He began with a series of belches,
that grew progressively louder;
but, try as he might, Hunn fell short of his
one hundred eighteen and one-tenth decibel record.

Bibhuti Bhushan Nayak's new mark bettered by one brick
the current "groin break" record
held by American Cliff Flenoy.
On this same occasion, Nayak broke yet another record
for the most pushups in a minute—one hundred thirty-three—
outdoing the mark of one hundred sixteen
set by Paul Dean, a Briton.

   Huzza
Wolfgang Kulov's underwater journey
went without incident: "A couple of fish," he said,
"came along for the ride, sitting on the handlebars."
And at one point, he had to drive around
a discarded garden gnome that someone had thrown in the water.
"But other than that," Kulov said, "no major incidents arose."

Samir Tandon achieved his expertise through practice
by reciting texts backwards up to twelve hours every day
for a period of four years. "I have always wanted
to do things differently," he explained.

Tandon, who has added English pop songs to his repertoire,
next wants to produce and sell
audio and video cassettes of his performances.
"And," Tandon added, "I would love to publicly read
a book written by a great writer in reverse."

Paul Hunn admitted disappointment
at his failure to set a new burping record
but vowed that he would return with another challenge
when he was feeling in better form.
"Hunn was under a lot of pressure with everyone watching,"
said Guinness Records senior researcher Della Howe.
"But," she noted, "It's like the athletes
at the Commonwealth Games. . . .
you have to train hard and just go for it.".

Bibhuti Bhushan Nayak's "groin break" and pushup feats
were recorded by local newspapers and by a TV crew.
They will be submitted for ratification by the *Guinness Book*,
where his name has already been entered for completing
eight hundred nineteen backhand pushups , the most ever.
He also holds records for performing
one thousand four hundred forty-eight situps in an hour,
and for withstanding forty-three kicks to the groin.

   Excelsior
Wolfgang Kulov had thought his feat would take him
at least eight hours, so he was amazed
when he emerged from the water
after only three hours and fifteen minutes.
But setting a world record for underwater cycling
was not something Kulov had ever expected
to have any difficulty doing. "As far as I know,"
he said, "I am the first person
to ever have ridden a bike underwater."

Samir Tandon admitted that learning to recite backwards
"was difficult in the beginning.
My family members thought I was mad
and forbade me from taking up the hobby.
But, nowadays," he said, "when they see me perform,
they are proud and happy.
In fact they encourage me."

Paul Hunn got a similar response to burping out loud.
"My dad used to hate it when I did it as a kid," he said,
"but he is coming round to the idea now.
My girlfriend wasn't too keen at first either," Hunn added,
"but when we went out to America
to appear on a chat show there,
she soon came round."

Bibhuti Bhushan Nayak, as a child,
Was inspired to break records
after seeing a television series on human endurance.
"These acts," he explained, "are not only
very strenuous, but also
extremely dangerous." However, he stressed,
"nothing can be achieved without risks.
I want to break other records," Nayak added,
"I want to aim higher."

Hart's Neck Haibun

Book III: 2002

July 26

To Bayview or to Cappy's Chowder House? To Cod End or to
the Fiddlehead? To Harbor View or to King Eider's Pub? To the
Mariners or to Pine Cone Café? To Puffin's Nest or to Restaurant
at the Navigator? To Rockland Café or to Schooner Fare? To Sunset
Terrace or to the Landings? To the Dip Net or to the Harpoon?
To the Haven or to the Helm? To the Offshore or to the Sea Gull?
To the Wooden Peg or to the Waterworks? To Wayfarer East or to
Windows at the East Wind Inn?

July 27

Wake of lobster boat
heading out of harbor
lifts and drops
the floating dock,
turns the gangplank's
shadow into an
undulating
water snake.

July 28

At Art's Lobsters Inc., *twist off the large claws and crack open with a
nutcracker, pliers, knife or rock.*

At Bay Lobster Co., *separate the tail from the body and break off the tail
flippers.*

At Miller's Lobster Co., *insert a fork and push the tail meat out in one piece.*

At Oyster River Lobster, *remove and discard the black vein which runs the entire length of the tail meat.*

At Shaw's Fish & Lobster Warf, *the meat lies in four pockets (or joints) where the small walking legs are attached.*

At Ship to Shore Lobster Co., *the small walking legs contain excellent meat.*

At Waterman's Beach Lobster, *the small walking legs contain excellent meat, which can be removed by sucking on the ends.*

July 29

"WILL SWAP 100 PAPERBACK WESTERNS FOR 100 OF YOURS."

July 30

Hand painted sign posted in front yard:

> *Cottages Watched*
> *Monuments Restored*

"So, what's your line of work?"
"Watching cottages. But right now, I'm on my lunch break. Shortly, I'll have to get back to my job: sitting on this porch . . . rocking in this chair . . . keeping both eyes open."

July 31

> Sign painted on the side of a truck
> hauling Port-a-Potty: "Blow Bros."
>
> (Could one of them
> be named Joe?)

Their slogan:
"Number One in the
Number Two Business."

August 1

NEWS RADIO 1040
Scientists report
that gene therapy
could repair
broken hearts

*

MIDEAST TALKS END IN FAILURE
Good news for war buffs.

*

MISS AMERICA TO SHOWCASE
MORE SKIN, LESS TALENT.
Hubba! Hubba!

August 2

"Lost & Found: 12 ft. blue aluminum jon boat, Earl's Girl, lost in
Broad Cove, Cushing.
Reg. # NH5665AY. Call 354-6431"

August 3

Thomaston Police Blotter:
" . . . 100 incidents including eight agency assists, three animal
problems, one assault, one all-terrain vehicle problem, one car
and deer accident, eight check-ins and three citizen assists . . .
one criminal mischief complaint, one custodial interference, one
disorderly conduct complaint, one domestic assault, one erratic

vehicle, one complaint of harassment, one intoxicated person, and one juvenile problem."

August 4

One block beyond
cannery row houses
stands the A & P
which to enter
is to step
back into childhood—
mine—Buffalo,
circa 1955.

Displayed on rack:
toy cars, pressed
tin cap guns
with lever action
and rolls of caps,
red with black
powder dots—
two for a quarter.

Teenage girl
at checkout
hefts a toddler
on her hip,
another child,
standing, tugs
 at her pant leg,
"Mommy,
Mommy!"

Large woman
behind me in line
nods in Gianni's
direction, asks,
"Your grandson?"

August 5

Tear-smudged eyeshadow
or traces of a black eye?

August 6

Rockland Police Blotter:
" . . . summons for unnecessary acceleration noise,
a fine of $126."

" . . . summons for and failure to produce a driver's license,
a fine of $172."

" . . . summons for inadequate headlamp on a bicycle,
a fine of $63."

". . . summons for negotiating a worthless instrument,
a fine of $50."

August 7

WILD WEST WINS AT MOOSEBEC REACH LOBSTER BOAT
RACES
— *Maine Coastal News*

When you say lobster boat racing
the first place that comes to mind
has to be Beals Island/Jonesport.

Signup started around 0800
and stretched past 1000.
However the main concern was fog
that had been thick all morning.

The race committee just kept hoping
the fog would lift and just about 1030
their prayers were answered. It cleared

from the bridge to the
eastern end of the reach.

In the four Work Boat classes
34 boats went to the line.
In Class A, Matthew Alley's **Britt & Matt II**,
(Libby 16, powered with a 25-hp Mercury outboard),
continued their winning ways from last year.

In Class B, eleven boats
crossed the starting line,
With Nick Wiberg's **Shit Happens**
(Holland 14, 55-hp outboard)
grabbing first place.

For the last race of the day,
"Fastest Lobster Boat Afloat,"
just two boats opted to make the run
with **Wild Wild West**
beating **First Team.**

*

Seventy-four-year-old Andrew Gove, of Stonington,
who has raced for twenty years,
holds the current record of 51.3 miles per hour
for the fastest diesel-powered working lobster boat.

He says the sport keeps him on his toes,
and gives him fresh ideas
for staying at the top of the fishing game
and making his boat, **Uncle's UFO,**
more efficient for hauling his 800 lobster traps.

"When you get up past 74,
it's hard to be competitive," Gove said.
"I've got some lame arms and legs.
I've worked hard all my life.

I've fished for over 50 years.
I go year round, according to the weather, 'course.
I wanted to have a little fun out of it before I die."

"It's just a Down East tradition," said Arvin Young,
who has also competed in the annual races for decades.
"We would race scows if we had to."

August 8

"They come here on vacation or whatever and they say, 'Oh, what a wonderful place to live.' And then they move here and they discover that, oh, God, there's all this noise. The lobster boats are going out early in the morning! The fish bait stinks! The lobster traps are unsightly because when they haul them up and they sit out they start stinking. Funny thing is these people have moved here to get away from it all and the first thing they do when they get here is try to change it to be the way it was where they came from."

Notes:

"twist off the large claws . . . " —from instructions printed on Lobster table mats)

"WILL SWAP . . . " —*Rockland Free Press,* classifieds

"MIDEAST TALKS END IN FAILURE" —*Boston Globe* headline

"MISS AMERICA TO SHOWCASE . . . "—*Rockland Courier Gazette* headline

"Lost & Found . . . " —*Rockland Free Press*

"When you say lobster boat racing . . . "— *Maine Coastal News*

"They come here on vacation . . . "— conversation with Richard Stanley, son of legendary Southwest harbor boat builder Ralph W. Stanley as quoted in *The Lobster Coast,* Colin Woodward

Protective and Defensive Devices

"PROTECTIVE AND DEFENSIVE DEVICES"

From a collage by Tuli Kupferberg

*"In honor of his fourth anniversary as police commissioner,
Howard Leary received a paperweight model of a nightstick from
the Mayor."*

— *New York Daily News*

Peerless handcuffs.
Precision American made,
tempered steel, double safety lock, 2 keys.
Model: *Subpoena.*

Leg irons.
Kick proof, pick proof, and run proof.
Model: *Irons.*

Handcuff transport belt.
Restrains prisoner
by keeping hands safely at waist.
Model: *Restrict.*

Twister chain & holder.
Easy to apply;
uses pressure as needed to subdue.
Model: *Safeguard.*

Judo stick.
Unbreakable plastic persuader—defensive item.
Rubber for sure grip.
Used to persuade or subdue the unruly prisoner.
Model: *Judo.*

Midget thumb cuffs.
Off-duty,
especially good for juveniles.
Model: *Spy.*

Aluminum knuckles.
Light cast aluminum,
carries nicely in pocket,
fits hand comfortably.
Model: *Slugger.*

Palm slapper.
Concealed in palm, powder loaded lead persuader.
Fits easy in pocket.
Model: *Rowdy.*

Lead loaded sap gloves.
Handsome, flexible dress glove
made of genuine deerskin.
You would never know this is loaded
with 6 oz. powdered lead saps, built-in.
Black only.
Model: *Saboteur.*

Fully Automatic

"This is still a dangerous world. It's a world of madmen and uncertainty and potential mential-losses."

—Texas Governor George W. Bush

Still squeezing off single rounds?

At the Texas Gun and Knife Show,
the "Hell Fire Triggers" kit
can be purchased
for the special "event" price
of $19.95.

Convert your semi

"It's a great stress reliever,"
promoter James Hulinger says.
"It's like bowling.
If you had a bad
day at work, just
load up
and let go."

*Convert your semi and discover
the pleasures of fully automatic.*

EAST-WEST DIALOGUE 2002

For Barbara Kruger

Russian Worker and American Worker

R: What are these "perks" for American business executives I keep reading about in my newspaper?

A: Short for "perquisites," meaning lavish rewards given for earning their companies big profits.

R: But what do they consist of? Cuban cigars? Beluga caviar? Fine French champagnes?

A: Much more: lifetime leases to Manhattan luxury apartments; limousines to chauffeur their children to school; private boxes at the Metropolitan Opera and Yankee Stadium; corporate jets to fly them to Wimbledon or to Biarritz, where they're put up at 4-star hotels; on top of all that, unlimited expense accounts so, if they wish, they can order Cuban cigars, Beluga caviar and the best champagne.

R: It was the same in my country in the old days under communism.

A: How's that?

R: Back then, the managers who ran our state-owned enterprises lived in secluded compounds away from ordinary workers. They had vacation dachas at the best resorts on the Black Sea. Forest preserves were set aside where only they were allowed to hunt. They drove Mercedes, smoked Cuban cigars, ate the most expensive Beluga caviar, and drank fine French champagnes.

A: So it was the same.

R: Yes, and all paid for by the workers.

A: In America, it's not only the employees but also the company stockholders, and the consumers, who pay.

R: But under capitalism don't the executives already get big salaries?

A: In America, the CEO earns a thousand times more than the average worker.

R: Such extravagance! How do American businesses keep thriving?

A: Many have gone bankrupt.

R: In my country the whole system was bankrupt. Finally, it collapsed.

A: And what happened to the workers?

R: We now sell pencils on the street corner or trade bootleg CDs on the black market.

A: In America, when a company goes bottom up, the workers lose not only their jobs but also the money they've put aside for retirement.

R: And those at the top who were responsible—were they thrown out? Made to pay back the "perks" they had taken?

A: They lost their jobs but retired with their pockets stuffed with money to live in mansions the size of the White House.

R: It was the same in my country.

A: Do you mean that after the collapse of communism, the managers retired to mansions?

R: Their jobs were gone but not the wealth they had accumulated.

A: And what's become of them?

R: They have started up private companies under Russia's new free enterprise system.

A: Ah! We have an American expression for this: "Business as usual!"

ACE

I pulled the trigger at two and a half miles.
The missile impacted him . . . it was a MIG-21.
It was tan, and on fire.
—1998 interview with Gulf War veteran Lieutenant
Commander Nicholas "Mongo" Mongillo, the first Navy
pilot since 1968 to shoot down a MIG from a single-seat
fighter.

I was given the Silver Star.
The only awards higher than that for combat
are the Medal of Honor and the Navy Cross.

I don't want to become a braggart.
If someone asks me about the shootdown,
I'm more than happy to talk about it,
but I've never been one
to actively put it out there.
I'm a proven commodity.
I've got 25 missions in combat.
I've shot down a plane.
Been there, done that.

You look at the way
Mark McGwire handles himself,
he's a very likable guy; he's like,
"Hey, I'm glad it happened to me."
He did something really great, he knows it,
but he's not gonna rub it
in anyone's face.
He's thankful for it . . .
for the fans, everything.

I never hit 70 home runs
but, since my shootdown, I'd like to think

I handled myself
the same way,
with a little bit of humility.
For the Medal of Honor
you usually have to die.

21st Century Newsbriefs I

For Aaron McGruder

SOCIAL SECURITY REFORM TO TARGET WEALTHY RETIREES

Garden parties at country estates
next summer will be serving
domestic instead of
foreign vintage champagne.

*

PRESIDENT DECLARES WAR ON TERRORISM

As with the War on Poverty,
as with the War on Drugs,
a successful outcome
is guaranteed.

*

PRESIDENT CREDITED WITH INVIGORATING ECONOMY

Night and day,
at the South Bend, Indiana, A. M. General factory,
new Humvees roll off the assembly line,
painted shades of sand.

*

DEFENSE SECRETARY CALLS FOR LEANER ARMY

Generals dining in the Pentagon's cafeterias
favored the Beef Stroganoff entrée—
but now made with yogurt,
substituting for the sour cream.

*

JOBS OUTLOOK IMPROVING

Bricklayers, stonemasons, carpenters are in demand;
plumbers, electricians are working overtime—
prison construction
is an American growth industry!

HART'S NECK HAIBUN

Book IV: 2003

July 27

Poised
on stilts,
motionless
in mudflats,

" 'sdat chu,
Great Blue
Heron?"

"A-huh. A-huh."

July 28

After fog, rain,
heavy, lasting all night
into this early morning:

an endless herd
of toy ponies
stampeding
overhead.

Now squirrels
cavorting
on the plank
and tar paper
roof!

Don't kid yourself.

Wind
has shaken
drops loose
from the firs'
rain-laden
boughs.

July 29

More threat of rain today so we head inland by car to Elmer's Barn:

"If you want to see the most unusual antique shop in New England YOU GOT TO VISIT ELMER'S BARN, Coopers Mills, Maine. . . . Go slow when you get close, Coopers Mills is easy to miss. We're so small that the politicians have to stick their hands in their own pockets."

"Hi! I'm Elmer."

"I put this picture in so you could see
I ain't the two-headed idiot the neighbors say I am."

"I have the most unusual antique shop in Maine. There's three floors of chairs, picture frames, clocks, trunks, brass beds, and wood stoves for starters. I will buy and sell all house contents. We also have stuff here you've never seen before and will never see again. Last year we sold a stuffed zebra, two mooseheads, a player piano, and a totem pole. If you want it I can get it if I ain't got it already."

Elmer is enthroned near the first floor entrance in an old chair, usually accompanied by a male crony, exchanging local gossip and news, and trading wry banter with any visitor who will engage him. A tourist vacationing in Damariscotta, up from North Carolina, wants to buy a metal "sculpture" but asks if Elmer can hold it until he is ready to return home, as he doesn't want to lug it about while on vacation. Elmer asks what he does for a living (no doubt to gauge how to negotiate the price, later). The man says, "I'll give you three guesses." "A teacher?" Elmer says. "No, I'm not a teacher, but I take that as a compliment," the man answers. "I didn't mean it," Elmer shoots back, "as a compliment."

July 30

Who drew this
gauze curtain?

The neighbor's cabin,
the towering pine

have become
silhouette cutouts

framed and hung
on the wall where

once there was
a window.

July 31

Muffled horn
announcing
    Fog
        Fog
at dawn, at dusk,
and through the night
has banished the
"*You*

ah you"
of mourning doves.

Eaves of the cottage roof
drip-drip,
drip,
at dawn, at dusk,
and through the night.

August 1

The used, much abused Oldtown canoe sitting on the front lawn
at a Thomaston yard sale ($100), and, later, the same battered
vintage canoe, in serious need of patching, on display at Elmer's
Barn ($650). R. Mutt would have a field day at Elmer's Barn.
(Mary: "Elmer would put a price sticker on a used toothbrush and
try to sell it for a dollar.")

*

The thrill
of this paddle
is the exploration
and dramatic
turns,

you never know
what you will
see around the
next bend:

wild turkey,
deer,
mallards,
goldfinches.

How far can you go
before water depth
and deadfall
turn you back?

Head out
with the tide
on a downhill
rush to the sea.

The challenge
is holding back
the speed
just enough

so that
you can
turn your craft
in time

to avoid
a nose plant
into the sinuous
oxbows.

*

How many times have you driven by
Sherman Lake Rest Area
adjacent to Route 1 in Edgecomb
and wondered how the paddling is
on Sherman Lake?

Well, it's even
better
than you imagined.

Notes:

."If you want to see the most unusual antique shop . . . "—brochure for Elmer's Barn

Note:

R. Mutt: Duchamp's signature on his Readymade urinal sculpture, "Fountain."

"You

      ah you"—Lorine Niedecker

"The thrill . . . "—*Maine Sunday Telegram*

Leading by Example

ALL THE NEWS—SEPTEMBER 23, 2001

Q: Why aren't there any Wal-Marts in Afghanistan?
A: Because they're all Targets.
                                        —Popular American joke, 2001

According to the *Times*,
"Air Force bombers are heading
toward distant airfields
to fight a shadowy foe
flitting through the mountains
in a deeply hostile land
already so poor and so ruined
by two decades of war that it is
virtually bereft of targets."

"FORGET THE PAST,"
the headline instructs.
"IT'S A WAR UNLIKE ANY OTHER."

"INFINITE JUSTICE"

"Shortly after word spread among key military leaders that President
[George H.W.] Bush had ordered the invasion of Panama, Lieutenant
General Thomas Kelly, Operations Officer on the Joint Staff, received a
call from General James Lindsay, Commander-in-Chief (CINC), Special
Operations Command. His call did not concern some last-minute change
in the invasion plan; rather, it concerned a seemingly insignificant detail
of the operation: its name. 'Do you want your grandchildren to say you
were in Blue Spoon?' he asked. Lieutenant General Kelly agreed that
the name should be changed. After hanging up the phone, General Kelly
discussed alternatives with his deputy for current operations, Brigadier
General Joe Lopez.
　　　'How about Just Action?' Kelly offered.
　　　'How about Just Cause?' Lopez shot back."
　　　　　　　　　　　　　—Bob Woodward , *The Commanders*

News Item: September 21, 2001—One month before the invasion,
Defense Secretary Donald H. Rumsfeld announced that the code
name for U. S. military operations in Afghanistan would be
changed for a second time.

Operation Infinite Justice was the initial name.
Infinite Justice followed the practice
of using a single theme for a region
where Americans are at war.

For the Persian Gulf War
"desert" was the common denominator
as in Desert Shield, Desert Storm,
and subsequent or subordinate operations:
Desert Saber, the ground offensive;
Desert Farewell, the troop redeployment;
Desert Share, the distribution of leftover food to the US poor.
As Major General Charles McClain,
the Army's Chief of Public Affairs, wrote:
"The perception of an operation can be as important to success
 as the execution of that operation."

94

The theme for Afghanistan operations was "infinite."
The 1998 air assault on Osama Bin Laden's training camps,
for example, was called Operation Infinite Reach.
"It gave the impression," an official said,
"that there was no sanctuary for the terrorists."

After the September 11 attacks,
the president made justice his key theme.
Pentagon officials picked Infinite Justice
for the second operation in the "infinite" series.
But Islamic scholars raised objections. Only God
could mete out infinite justice, they complained.

Two Protestant clergy who specialize in ethical issues agreed.
They said the term "infinite justice" carries strong
            religious resonance,
suggesting divine sanction, and therefore was inappropriate
for a military campaign waged by a secular state.
"It's a sin of pride," one of them added.

In response, Pentagon officials dropped Infinite Justice
as the name for the Afghan campaign
and put in its place Operation Noble Eagle.

A similar problem arose with an Operation Masher
during the Vietnam War. President Johnson is reported
to have angrily complained to Army planners
that Masher sounded too bloodthirsty,
and did not reflect his theme of "pacification" in Vietnam.
As a result, Operation Masher was renamed White Wing.

Operation Enduring Freedom is the latest effort
to match the name of the Afghan war against terrorism
to the national mood. "'Enduring',"
said Defense Secretary Rumsfeld,
"suggests that this is not a quick fix."

Capsule History of Herat, Afghanistan

After the *mujahedeen* had defeated their Communist overlords,
the men of Herat took to the streets
behind their leader Ismail Khan,
chanting slogans and firing their rifles into the air.
The women of Herat, covered head to toe in *burkas*,
stood in doorways watching the celebration
through narrow eye slits.

Then, the "holy warriors" of Herat allied with the Taliban
to install Islamic rule over the country.
For two years they laid siege to the capital, Kabul.
After the last holdouts surrendered, the fighting men
returned home. They ran through the streets of Herat
shouting in celebration and firing their rifles into the air.
Covered head to toe in burkas, the women of Herat
stood in doorways watching through narrow eye slits.

Finally the Americans came. Their troops
chased the Taliban fighters back into the mountains
and established democratic rule throughout Afghanistan.
Now allied with the victors, the "holy warriors" of Herat
once again took to the streets chanting slogans
and firing their rifles into the air. Standing in doorways,
covered head to toe in *burkas*,
the women of Herat looked on through narrow eye slits.

21st Century Newsbriefs II—Embracing Values

Q: How do you play Taliban bingo?
A: B-1, F-16, A-4, C-130 . . .

—Late night TV joke

AGRICULTURAL PRODUCTION REBOUNDS

In fields that under the Taliban
were barren of all but landmines
cultivated flowers as far as the eye can see
now bend their heads in the breeze—
opium growing
is once again a thriving enterprise.

*

NATION BUILDING

Entire neighborhoods of California-style mansions
are replacing farmers' huts
on the outskirts of Kabul.

Government officials after work now relax
with family members watching
American sitcoms on satellite TVs.

*

EMBRACING AMERICAN VALUES

Outside the gates of the U. S. compound in Kabul,
lessons only recently learned
about freedom of speech and assembly
are being put to practice by Afghan students
shouting slogans and burning American flags.

*

VICTORY FOR DEMOCRACY

At polling stations in Kabul,
Afghanis were so thrilled by the novelty
of voting to choose their leaders

that after casting their ballots
many returned to the end of the line
to do it again.

In provincial towns, where women
are forbidden to go out in public,
husbands cast proxy votes for their wives;

and in remote areas,
villagers placed all their ballots
in the hands of the tribal leader
who chose the best candidate for them.

*

Coda

Popular Afghani joke, circa 2003:

Q: Why don't we suffer from the same ills as other poor nations?
A: Because, thanks to America, we got an injection of Vitamin B-52.

21st Century Newsbriefs III: Leading by Example

—For Dan Wasserman

COERCIVE INTERROGATION TECHNIQUES BARRED BY
MILITARY

Snarling attack dogs,
held, straining at leashes,
inches away from naked prisoners' faces,
will henceforth be muzzled.

*

IRAQIS VIEW AMERICANS AS LIBERATORS, SAYS PRESIDENT

Citizens gather daily in the streets of Iraqi cities
to dance and cheer in displays of gratitude
around smoldering Humvees.

*

ALLIES CITED FOR HUMAN RIGHTS ABUSES

Private jets that under CIA contract
ferry hooded passengers to undisclosed locations
have been issued flight plans
for new overseas destinations.

*

ARMY USES BANNED WEAPONS AGAINST IRAQI CIVILIANS

"Shake and Bake"—Army slang for white phosphorus bombs

Bringing American 4th of July fireworks displays
into Iraqi living rooms.

*

PENTAGON PAYS PUBLICISTS TO PLANT FAKE NEWS
FAVORABLE TO U.S. IN IRAQI NEWSPAPERS

Teaching freedom of the press
the American way.

*

U.S. TRAINED IRAQI POLICE ACCUSED OF PRISONER ABUSE

Imitation: the best form of flattery.

*

PRESIDENT CLAIMS THAT MANY ARE THANKFUL THE U.S.
IS IN IRAQ

Kim Jong-il, the leader of North Korea, no doubt;
and the leaders of Iran and Syria as well.

"SPECIAL FRIENDSHIP"

After bulletproof glass had been installed in the windows of the Prime Minister's residence

After Bobbies wearing Day-Glo jackets had been posted on street corners throughout London

After the roads and squares leading to the city center had been sealed off to traffic by agents of Scotland Yard

After barriers had been put in place to keep marchers and curious onlookers back out of camera view

After fighter-jets and helicopter gun ships had scoured the skies and after snipers had taken up positions on the rooftops

Then, under cover of darkness, the President's armored helicopter touched down behind Buckingham Palace

Then his limousine was rolled out onto the lawn and the Secret Service ushered the President into the armored Cadillac

Then, at dawn, his motorcade sped through the empty London streets to 10 Downing Street

There, the Prime Minister greeted him

There, he was escorted outside before gathered public officials and television reporters

There, he stepped to the podium set up on the lawn and spoke into the microphones

The President spoke of America's "special friendship" with the British people.

GOKTAPA

One Kurdish man, who escaped with his life,
returned three years after the gas attack,
seeking the remains of his son.

He found the body, undisturbed,
among reeds beside the river,
where the boy had crawled to die.

The flesh was gone,
but the father recognized
the belt and shirt
that still covered the bones.

And, in the shirt pocket,
the place where his son had always kept it,
he found the key
to the family tractor.

REGIME CHANGE

Ordinary lives have changed for the better.

For example, the sign painter Hamid al-Imari.
He used to make banners with slogans that proclaimed
"Happy Birthday Our Magnificent Leader."
Now, he paints billboards
that read "Drink Pepsi."

"A thriving start-up venture in democratic capitalism."

Before the American invasion,
cars used to line up for blocks
waiting for a turn at the gas pumps
only to find they had gone dry.

But now gasoline is on sale
in plastic gallon jugs
on every Baghdad street corner.

Under Saddam, many conducted their business
hidden from sight
out of fear for their lives.

But now they have emerged from dark alleyways—
prostitutes, for instance,
have become a common sight.

Iraqis already see a brighter future

Thamir Ghadhban, Director of Planning at the Ministry of Oil,
today sits behind a large wooden desk
with not one but four telephones upon it.

Once the service is restored,
he expects them to start ringing off their hooks.

Meanwhile, on the streets of Baghdad,
everyone carries a cell phone
in anticipation of the day
when the wireless networks will start working.

"Stuff happens"

The priceless art treasures and antiquities
thought to have been looted from museums
during the first days of Baghdad's liberation

have been found in safekeeping
locked inside vaults
belonging to Western collectors.

"Mission Accomplished"

Under Saddam, Iraqis citizens waited
outside police stations and prison compounds
hoping for information about family members
who had been abducted off the streets
or taken from their homes in the night.
Most were never heard of again,
their bodies secretly buried in unmarked graves.

But since the overthrow of Saddam, things are different.
Iraqis now know to go to the city morgue
to recover the bodies of their relatives who were killed
accidentally in crossfires or by stray ordinance.
And citizens of Baghdad line up every day now
outside the American military compound
where they receive cash compensation for family members
whose lives were lost at the hands of their liberators.

Historical Afterword:

"The Baghdad communiqués are belated, insincere, incomplete. Things have been far worse than we have been told, our administration more bloody and inefficient than the public knows. We are today not far from a disaster."—T. E. Lawrence (Lawrence of Arabia) writing in the *Sunday Times of London* on Aug. 22, 1920, about the British occupation of what was then called Mesopotamia.

Act I, 1994 headline:
U.S. MARINES INVADE HAITI, RESTORE ARISTIDE TO POWER

Act II, 2003 headline:
U.S. LAUNCHES "OPERATION IRAQI FREEDOM"

Entre Act, Overheard on a Boston bus

Have you read today's paper?
I bought a copy
of the New York Times.

The Times *is always*
good
when something
bad happens.

Act III, 2004 headline:
U.S. PRESSURES ARISTIDE TO RESIGN, FLEE HAITI; MARINES
DEPLOYED

Act IV, 2005 headline:
IRAQIS GO TO THE POLLS IN HISTORIC ELECTIONS

Epilogue:
Thanks to the American military intervention
that removed a brutal dictator from power,

Iraqis are now free to speak their minds
without fear of reprisal,

And to cast ballots for a slate
of handpicked leaders—

just as in Haiti.

HART'S NECK HAIBUN

Book V: 2004

July 28

> Time here measured
> by the movement
> of great blue herons
> stalking crabs
> in the shallows
> at low tide.

July 29

5:38 A.M., sun not yet up but the glow of dawn spread over all from the point of Hart's Neck. The lowest of low tides. You could walk across the harbor in places but for the muck that sucks your shoes off (I've tried it). Even the two children's dories at the far end of the neighbor's long pier and the floating dock they are always tethered to are today aground. One lobster pot, tied to its buoy, is only half submerged. A pair of great blue herons at water's edge pick their way among rocks and seaweed. A seagull shadows them, hoping for an invitation to breakfast, or at the very least an opportunity to clean up their scraps. Much thrumming of motors already, shouts of lobstermen hauling gear in preparation for the day's work. And now the sun is climbing the ladder of fir branches.

July 30

> Furze of chamomile
> & yellow clover
> along the shoulders
> of Hart's Neck Road.

Purple loosestrife
fills the ditches.
Clustered day lilies
front fieldstone walls.
Pink and white beach roses
line post and rail fences.

One field overgrown
with tansy, milkweed,
purple cowslip,
black-eyed Susans.
Another field
blowsy with chest-high
Queen Anne's lace.

And where only spiky
green moss grows
on tree-shaded lawns,
up poke yellow
chanterelle caps.

July 31

Overheard: "Ya know what lobstermen call kayakers, don't ya?
Speed bumps."

August 1

Twittering flight
of goldfinches
in, out, and
back through
juniper hedges,
weaving a
gilt thread
embroidery.

August 2

A father and his towhead three-or-so-year-old son ply the harbor off my porch bow in a weathered skiff, connecting the dots, buoy to buoy. Black lab seated in the prow, father at the oars, boy at the stern holding the painter of his yellow plastic tugboat with bright red cabin, which bobs and lurches in their wake. Father teaching son to haul and re-bait traps: he holds each lobster up for his son to size, drops one runt overboard, keeps the keepers.

August 3

> *Suitable for framing:*
> Perched on
> rocky rise
> lone house
> with steep pitched
> asphalt shingle roof
> widow's watch on top
> and a lone gull
> squat atop that
> taking in view of
> harbor, islands
> and sea beyond;
> roof's ridge
> drip-painted in guano.

August 4

Alice Knight, vice-president of this year's Lobster Festival has been directly involved with the event since she was a Sea Princess in 1951. Her daughter, Celia, was a Sea Princess in 1984, and her grandchildren will be pirates in the Children's Parade on August 4. . . .

Life as a Sea Princess back in the '50s was a little more glamorous than it is today, as Knight recalls it. The festival committee paid to have members of the press corps from all over New England come to Rockland for two weeks before the big event to photograph the princesses in silly hats and winsome poses and the photos went out to all the papers.

The reporters were, of course, fed lobster at every conceivable opportunity. During the three days of the festival, all of the princesses and their chaperones were housed in the old Rockland Hotel, overlooking the harbor. Convertibles were parked outside the hotel around the clock, ready to take them wherever they needed to go.

But, like Cinderella, once the festival was over, the royal treatment ended. "On Sunday," she said, "they dumped us." Knight's father, Ernest Crie, now 96 years old, remembers driving around town looking for Knight and one of her fellow princesses, and finding them wending their way home on foot after the days of being feted and driven about, each wearing a huge, shaggy straw hat bought at the carnival, each very weary.

—Rockland Free Press

August 5

James Salter writes in *Passionate Falsehoods* :"'Bologna,' Laura Betti said. ' . . . It's famous for three things. Its learning—it has the oldest university in Italy; its food; and lastly, its . . . ' Here she used the most common word describing fellatio.

"'It's a specialty,' she said. 'All the various forms are called by the names of pasta. Rigate, for instance, which is a pasta with thin, fluted marks. For that the girls gently use their teeth. When there used to be brothels, there was a Signorina Bolognese—that was her specialty.'"

A balding, forty-something man among the crowd at last year's Maine Lobster Festival in Rockland wore a T-shirt: "The More Hair I Lose, The More Head I Get."

August 6

A robin's-egg-blue sky, clear
but for one small charcoal cloudsmudge
over spruces along the cemetery ridge.

Get outta here!

That did it.
Now it's gone.

August 7

Crystal clear air and brilliant blue skies streaked with high wisps
of cloud for our last Maine day of this year. We go to Drift-In
Beach until high tide, then back to the cottage for a late lunch.
Kayak one last time around the harbor, collecting names of new
boats at anchor. Then drive off to the Lobster Festival in Rockland
to enjoy the carnival atmosphere. Later, driving back toward
the cottage at sunset, we are treated to a magnificent lavender
sky. We keep slowing the car as we ride down the spine of the
St. George peninsula. The view of slate-gray river and lavender-
changing-to-pink sky over sloping meadows dotted with baled
hay—breathtaking!

August 8

*. . . three horses, two dogs (Muggins and Sport), one carriage, three
cases of wine, two packages of stovepipe, two stoves, one iron pot,
four washstands, one barrel of hardwood, seventeen cots, seventeen
mattresses, four canvas packages, one buckboard, five large barrel, and
one half-barrel. Two tubs of butter, one bag of coffee, one chest of tea, a
crate of china, a dozen rugs, four milk cans, two drawing boards, twenty-
five trunks, thirteen small boxes, a boat, and a hamper. . . .*

Next summer we'll pack lighter!